2/17

CONNECT WITH ELECTRICITY

HOW TRANSISTORS WORK

BY JAMES ROLAND

LERNER PUBLICATIONS ◆ MINNEAPOLIS

To my father, Jim, who helped me build a
simple radio when I was young and went
on to help me in countless other ways, big
and small, for the rest of his life
—J.R.

Special thanks to content consultant Neal Clements, Adjunct Professor of
Electrical and Computer Engineering, North Dakota State University

Lerner Publications Company
A division of Lerner Publishing Group, Inc.
241 First Avenue North
Minneapolis, MN USA 55401

For reading levels and more information, look up this title at
www.lernerbooks.com.

Main body text set in Aptifer Slab LT Pro 12/18.
Typeface provided by Linotype AG.

Library of Congress Cataloging-in-Publication Data

Names: Roland, James.
Title: How transistors work / by James Roland.
Description: Minneapolis : Lerner Publications, 2016. | Series: Connect
    with electricity | Audience: Age 9–12. | Audience: Grade 4 to 6. |
    Includes bibliographical references and index.
Identifiers: LCCN 2015050788 (print) | LCCN 2016010888 (ebook) |
    ISBN 9781512407839 (lb : alk. paper) | ISBN 9781512410112 (eb pdf)
Subjects: LCSH: Transistors—Juvenile literature. |
    Electronics—Juvenile literature.
Classification: LCC TK7872.T73 R6155 (print) | LCC TK7872.T73 (ebook) |
    DDC 621.3815/28—dc23

LC record available at http://lccn.loc.gov/2015050788

Manufactured in the United States of America
1-39355-21167-3/9/2016

CONTENTS

Transistors allow your favorite video games to work.

INTRODUCTION

A computer chip is smaller than a fingernail. But it can contain more than a billion microscopic devices that are the keys to electronics, called transistors. Without transistors we wouldn't have video games, cell phones, and countless other electronic machines and gadgets. Not all transistors are microscopic. Some are big enough to hold in your hand while you build a radio or a robot.

Transistors can do two very important jobs in electrical circuits. They can act as amplifiers to increase or control the electric current in an electronic device. Transistors can also be switches, turning a current on or off or controlling how much current flows through a circuit.

Transistors may be the most important devices in electronics. They play a big part in computers, tablets, cars, satellites, household appliances, and electric toys big and small. The more you know about them, the more you'll understand why the world relies on them in almost every modern electronic machine.

CHAPTER ONE

TRANSISTORS: UNSUNG HEROES OF MODERN ELECTRONICS

Think of any device that uses electricity. Chances are there's a transistor in there. Or maybe thousands or millions or even billions of transistors at work. It could be a remote-controlled helicopter or a school bus or a laptop computer. Almost every electronic machine that's more complicated than a flashlight contains a circuit with a transistor to help control the electric current running through that circuit.

To understand why transistors are so important, you need to know a little about how circuits work. A circuit is a path for an electric current to take from one end of a power source, such as a battery, all the way back to the other end of the power source. Along the way, the current in that circuit can turn on a TV, keep a hoverboard rolling, or make a doorbell ring. Transistors can control the current in a circuit automatically based on the different designs of the transistor and the circuit. Transistors are efficient because they don't need someone to switch them on and off.

A circuit may use one or many transistors. The transistors in this circuit are the small black boxes with three prongs in the lower left of this photo.

When voltage is applied and the transistor is on, electricity will flow through the transistor and out to the rest of the circuit. This is like a light switch being in the On position. When the transistor is off, no current flows through the transistor and the circuit voltage drops. This could be considered the Off position. By controlling the flow of electricity in this way, a transistor can be used as a switch.

VOLTAGE VS. CURRENT

The more you learn about transistors and circuits, the more you'll hear about electric current and voltage. Current is the amount of electricity moving through a circuit at a given time. Voltage is the pressure in the circuit that moves the current. Think of electricity, or an electric charge, as water moving from a holding tank down through a pipe. The current is the amount of water flowing inside the pipe. The voltage is the pressure that pushes the water through the pipe. Sometimes just a little voltage is all that's needed to get current moving through a transistor.

Some transistors, like a bipolar transistor, can also take
a small electric current and use it to turn on a bigger one.
In a complicated circuit, one component, such as a resistor,
may release a small amount of electric current. But another
component, such as a lightbulb, may need a larger current to
work. A transistor can make that happen. Another common use of
transistors is to make quiet sounds seem much LOUDER! This is
called amplification. A transistor radio, for example, can receive
radio signals through the air and convert them into electrical
signals that move through a transistor or several transistors.
The signals are amplified to come out of a speaker at whatever
volume you want.

MANAGING A CURRENT

So how does one little part of a circuit do all this boosting and
switching of electric currents? You might expect transistors to be
complicated machines. But actually, they're fairly simple.

The three main parts of a common bipolar transistor are called
the collector, the emitter, and the base. Those parts are

Transistor radios are
small radio receivers that
use transistors. After the
development of the transistor,
these radios became the
most popular electronic
communication devices of the
1960s and 1970s.

DIAGRAM OF A TRANSISTOR

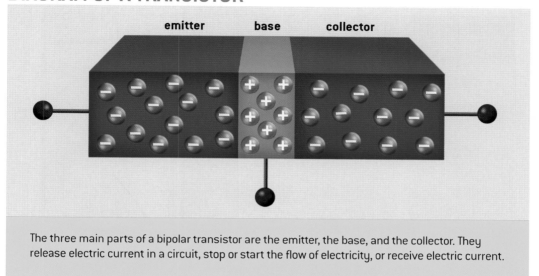

emitter   base   collector

The three main parts of a bipolar transistor are the emitter, the base, and the collector. They release electric current in a circuit, stop or start the flow of electricity, or receive electric current.

also called the source, the drain, and the gate in another type of transistor known as a field-effect transistor. In a bipolar transistor, the collector, as you might guess, collects or receives electric current. The emitter releases current. The base can stop or start the current flow. It can also help control how much current passes through the transistor. If you think back to the pipe running down from the water tank, the base is like the valve that controls how much, if any, water is released.

Transistors need to be made of semiconductor material to allow electricity to move. Silicon is one type of semiconductor material. It's also used to make computer chips.

In electronics, materials are defined by how easy or how difficult it is for an electric current to pass through them. In a conductor, for example, electricity can travel very easily.

SOLVE IT!

HOW HEARING AIDS WORK

When people start to lose their hearing, a hearing aid can be an amazing help. It sends sounds through little speakers so that people can hear them clearly. Do you think transistors in hearing aids work as amplifiers, or do they work as switches that the wearer controls to boost sounds? *(The answer key is on page 35.)*

Copper is a great conductor. So is water that hasn't been purified. That's why you always have to be careful with anything electric near water.

The opposite of a conductor is an insulator. Rubber and plastic are good insulators. It's almost impossible for electricity to pass through those materials. You'll see rubber and plastic coverings around wires and other parts of electronic equipment that conduct electricity. In between a conductor and an insulator is a semiconductor. This material can transfer

Many wires that are built into houses are covered in rubber tubing to protect electricians from shock.

an electric current in certain situations, such as if other elements or chemicals have been added to the semiconductor. This is called doping. Semiconductors can also transfer electric current if their temperature is at a certain level.

LEARN ABOUT LAYERS

Electric current is the movement of electrons through a circuit. Electrons are particles that help make up atoms. Atoms are the extremely tiny building blocks of everything around us.

The silicon used to make a transistor has to be doped to get electrons to move through the transistor the right way. Engineers can make silicon pick up more free-floating electrons by adding elements such as arsenic to a layer of the transistor. Because electrons are negatively charged, this layer is called negative type, or n-type. If you add different elements to another layer of the transistor, it picks up fewer free electrons.

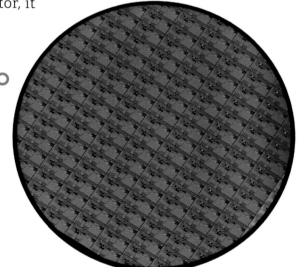

This material, known as a wafer, is a thin slice of a semiconductor like silicon. Wafers are used in certain types of circuits.

KNOW YOUR MODES

Transistors operate in one of four different modes. Each mode describes the flow of the current inside the transistor. These are the four operation modes:

- Saturation. The transistor's On position. Current flows easily from the collector to the emitter.
- Cutoff. The Off position. No current is traveling through the transistor.
- Active. A transistor at its most powerful. It amplifies by boosting the current coming in at the collector with a current coming in at the base so that the current can pass out of the emitter.
- Reverse-active. The opposite of active mode. Current comes in at the emitter and moves through the collector. This is rarely used for most transistors.

Then it's considered a positive type, or p-type. It has openings that will attract electrons from the n-type. That's what gets the current moving.

Two different types of semiconductors touching each other in a transistor creates a junction. That's the part of a transistor that connects p-type and n-type semiconductors. Electrons will flow from the n-type to the p-type across the junction. The arrangement of the n-type and p-type layers in a transistor is one way of affecting the type of job a transistor can do. And because we ask transistors to do a lot of different tasks, we need more than one kind of transistor.

CHAPTER TWO

TYPES OF TRANSISTORS

Transistors differ in how they're designed and built. But all transistors act as a switch or an amplifier.

BIPOLAR TRANSISTOR

A bipolar transistor is a commonly used transistor, especially in amplifier circuits. Sometimes it's called a bipolar junction transistor. It looks like one you might find in a build-it-yourself radio kit. The collector, emitter, and base look like rods extending out of a square case.

It's called a bipolar transistor because of the two types of semiconductor material: n-type and p-type. One kind of bipolar transistor has two layers of n-type semiconductor material on either side of a layer of p-type material. This is known as an NPN type. It can amplify a signal by taking in current at the base, which controls the current moving from the collector to the emitter. The base receives a smaller electric current than comes in through the collector. The base passes that energy to the emitter. This turns on the transistor and allows current to flow from the collector to the emitter. So the smaller current received by the base can control what happens to the larger current picked up by the collector.

A PNP transistor has two layers of p-type semiconductor material on either side of an n-type layer. It does the opposite of an NPN transistor. It moves current from the emitter to the collector. The design of the circuit may affect which type of bipolar transistor should be used. In general, NPN transistors are more widely used because they have better performance. N-types have greater electron mobility than p-types. Mobility refers to how quickly electrons move through the semiconductor material. Greater mobility results in faster-operating circuits.

PNP AND NPN BIPOLAR TRANSISTORS

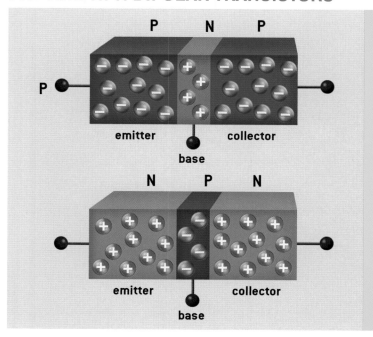

There are two types of bipolar transistors. An NPN transistor amplifies a signal by moving current from its collector to its emitter, while a PNP transistor does so by moving current from its emitter to its collector.

FIELD-EFFECT TRANSISTOR

Along with a bipolar transistor, the other most commonly used transistor is a field-effect transistor. It's often used to amplify wireless communications signals, such as those used by cell phones or radios. The way it works depends on the effect of the electric field or voltage that powers it. The flow of electrons in particular semiconductor materials can also affect how a transistor works. The three main parts of a field-effect transistor are called the source, drain, and gate. They act mostly the same way as an

FIELD-EFFECT TRANSISTOR

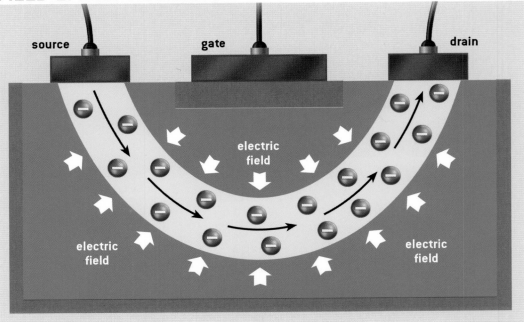

A field-effect transistor works similarly to a bipolar transistor. But unlike a bipolar transistor, which uses a small amount of current to control a larger amount of current, a field-effect transistor uses changes in voltage to control the current.

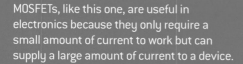

emitter, collector, and base in a bipolar transistor.

There is a special type of field-effect transistor called a metal-oxide-semiconductor field-effect transistor (MOSFET). It's especially useful as a power amplifier and a high-speed switch. Because a MOSFET can operate with low power, it's commonly used in computers, calculators, robotic toys, and other devices.

Perhaps the main difference between a bipolar transistor and a field-effect transistor is how they are controlled. A bipolar transistor is called a current-controlled device. The current it passes from collector to emitter depends on the base current that it receives. A field-effect transistor is a voltage-controlled device. That means even a small change in gate voltage can lead to a great change in the current from the source to the drain.

TRANSISTORS IN COMPUTERS

Some of the very first transistors were about as big as your palm. But they kept getting smaller and smaller. This helped computers get smaller and smaller too. Most transistors that are manufactured these days are too small to see. That's because these microscopic devices are at the heart of integrated circuits.

SOLVE IT!

LED READING LIGHT

You've built a simple, battery-powered circuit that includes a sensor. In the dark, the sensor sends a signal to light up a light-emitting diode, or LED. You want to use the LED as a reading light, but you realize the light could be brighter. What could you add to your circuit that might boost the light's power? *(The answer key is on page 35.)*

Integrated circuits are better known as microchips, or computer chips. The number of transistors packed into integrated circuits has grown to where more than a billion transistors can fit into a computer chip smaller than a postage stamp.

The more transistors you can squeeze into an integrated circuit, the greater your computer's memory. Memory has instructions for how the computer operates. It's also the storage space your computer uses to process information. The greater the memory, the more complex the tasks your computer can perform.

Integrated circuits, also known as computer chips, or microchips, store and process a computer's information.

OTHER TRANSISTOR DESIGNS

Some transistors are defined by their job, such as these:

- **Small signal transistors** amplify low-frequency radio signals.
- **Small switching transistors** are used primarily as switches in motors and other devices. They can also amplify radio signals. However, they can't produce the amount of amplification that small signal transistors can.
- **Power transistors** use a metal heat "sink" to move extra energy away from the rest of the transistor when a lot of current and voltage is used. They handle high voltages and high currents.
- **High-frequency transistors** are like small signal transistors, but they operate at higher frequencies.
- **Phototransistors** respond to light, which replaces the base or gate connection. They are used for devices such as security systems and some toys.

Power transistors, like this one, can handle high voltages.

Computers store information using a system of ones and zeros. When transistors are on and current is flowing through them, they are represented by a number 1. When they are off, they're represented by the number 0. All letters and numbers are represented by unique combinations of 1s and 0s. A capital Z, for example, is stored in this language as 01011010. This coded system of only two symbols was developed because the switches, or transistors, in a computer can be on or off.

Think about a computer with several microchips, each one with millions or billions of transistors. That's a lot of 1s and 0s. More important, it represents a lot of time-saving work that the computer can do for you. You may be using a computer to write a

Computers store information in sets of ones and zeros. Each set of ones and zeros is a code of instructions for a computer to follow.

report or solve a math problem or find information on the Internet. However you use it, the computer operates by switching many transistors on and off. The more transistors you have switching on and off, the faster your computer can operate and the more things it can do.

CHAPTER THREE

TRANSISTORS TRANSFORM ELECTRONICS

Have you ever seen old pictures of a family listening to a giant radio in their home? Or have you watched an old movie that featured a science lab with big glass tubes that had glowing lights inside them? Those were vacuum tubes. And that same kind of technology was also inside those big radios. Even the first computers used vacuum tubes.

Vacuum tubes are glass tubes that have had all gases removed from them. In 1883 Thomas Edison discovered that an electric current could run from a heated wire or filament at one end of a vacuum tube through empty space to a small metal plate at the other

In the 1930s and 1940s, families were entertained by listening to huge radios.

Thomas Edison is famous for many inventions and scientific breakthroughs. His discovery that electric current could be made to flow through a vacuum tube led to many other discoveries and inventions.

end. The discovery that an electric current could be made to flow in one direction in a vacuum tube without wires pushed other scientists to action. For example, inventor Lee de Forest added a metal grate in the middle of the tube to help control the current. During the next few decades, vacuum tubes were used to amplify currents in many electronic devices, especially radios and the earliest computers.

Vacuum tubes did much the same job that transistors do but not as quickly or easily. Vacuum tubes were big, clumsy, and breakable. They also produced a great amount of heat. So they were often at risk of burning out and needing replacement. They weren't always reliable, but they were extremely important in the early days of radio communication and computer science.

Scientists and engineers recognized the limitations of vacuum tubes and looked for better devices. Among them was Mervin Kelly. He was the head of research and later president at Bell Laboratories in New Jersey. Kelly thought that semiconductors might be the key to replacing vacuum tubes. After World War II (1939–1945), he assigned a scientist named William Shockley to lead a team at Bell Labs to develop a semiconductor switch. Two other important members of that

WHY IS IT CALLED A TRANSISTOR?

You might be familiar with the word *resistor*. Sounds a little like *transistor*, doesn't it? That's because the two devices do a similar job: control the flow of electric current through a circuit. The thickness and length of the wires in a resistor limit the current to just the right amount needed to run all the parts of the circuit. A transistor also controls the current, either as a switch or an amplifier. *Transistor* is a combination of "transfer" and "resistor" because the devices transfer electrical signals.

From left: John Bardeen, William Shockley, and Walter Brattain working at Bell Laboratories in 1948

team were John Bardeen and Walter Brattain. All three men were brilliant scientists. They were also surrounded by other creative and hardworking scientists and engineers.

After a lot of trial and error, the first transistor was built in December 1947. It was made by Brattain and Bardeen. The transistor had thin strips of gold foil that just barely touched a piece of germanium. Germanium is a metallic element that is a semiconductor like silicon. When a current ran through one piece of gold foil, it changed the electron activity in the germanium.

Then a stronger current left the germanium and went through the second gold foil strip. The Bell Labs team had created a point-contact transistor. It was a major milestone in the history of electronics.

POINT-CONTACT TRANSISTOR

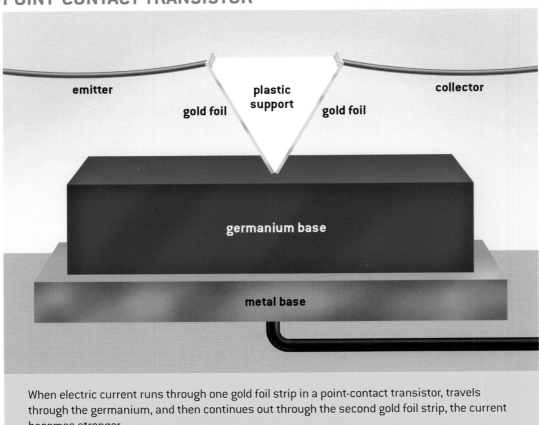

When electric current runs through one gold foil strip in a point-contact transistor, travels through the germanium, and then continues out through the second gold foil strip, the current becomes stronger.

Shockley was happy with the breakthrough the engineers on his team had made. But he was the team leader. He wanted to show that he could create something even better. For weeks Shockley tinkered with other semiconductor materials until he came up with what he nicknamed the sandwich. It also became known as a junction transistor. This design became the basis of the bipolar transistor.

Bell Labs called the device a transistor. It was announced to the public in June 1948. It didn't get much attention at the time. But soon transistors started being used in hearing aids, radios, and other products. Then people realized what a breakthrough Bell Labs had achieved. US companies mostly focused on military uses of transistors. But Japanese companies started mass-producing transistors for radios and other communications equipment. One of these companies would eventually become Sony in the 1950s.

In 1956 Shockley, Brattain, and Bardeen were awarded the Nobel Prize in Physics for their invention and development of the transistor. Shockley and several others who worked with him formed companies which, in the 1970s, came to be known as Silicon Valley. This area of western California is considered the heart of the United States' computer industry.

Before the Internet and widespread use of TV, getting news quickly to a lot of people could only happen through radios. Transistor radios allowed people to travel anywhere and still be connected to information. You can imagine how important those little handheld radios became to people around the world.

Jack Kilby poses with his invention, the very first integrated circuit, at the 1985 Science Exposition in Tsukuba, Japan.

Soon after the invention of the transistor, two engineers named Jack Kilby and Robert Noyce figured out a way to make transistors more efficient for computers. Instead of building transistors one by one, they proposed building several transistors on the same chip, along with the other parts of the circuit. Kilby and Noyce worked for different companies, but their combined research and designs would eventually be known as the integrated circuit. In 2000 Kilby won the Nobel Prize in Physics for his part in the invention of the integrated circuit.

When Kilby and Noyce were working on their designs in the 1950s, they could only dream about how computers and the transistors inside them would change the world. You probably don't go a day without using something that has a transistor, whether it's a computer, TV, electronic toy, or a car or bus that you ride in. You may not see transistors, but they're there, keeping electricity moving in just the right way so all those devices keep working.

CHAPTER FOUR

THE FUTURE OF TRANSISTORS

Since you know where transistors started, you might wonder where they're headed. Imagine a transistor so small it could be powered by one electron. It's not a crazy idea. Scientists and engineers are always working on shrinking transistors to smaller sizes.

Engineers are working to fit even more transistors into integrated circuits. Those computer chips could hold more memory or do more complicated tasks than ever before. Researchers also want to use materials other than silicon. Some modern materials may allow for faster electron movement than a semiconductor made of silicon.

Instead of limiting transistors to On or Off positions, perhaps in-between positions could be added. So instead of just 1 and 0, we could have code that uses 2, 3, 4, and so on. Then computers could work on many more computations at once than modern computers can. Computers could become much faster with these changes.

Engineers are constantly working to update electronics and make them more efficient. One way of doing this would be to create smaller transistors.

There are some concerns, however, such as how to keep a single electron from slipping right through the transistor. Then it might not charge the transistor the way that many electrons in electric current do. Scientists are working to make a single-electron transistor practical so that it wouldn't lose its charging abilities. Some researchers are looking into developing traps to keep the electrons in the right place.

Super-small transistors and other microscopic computer parts are examples of nanotechnology. That technology operates at the atomic level. Machines and parts at that level are so small you'd have a hard time believing they're really there.

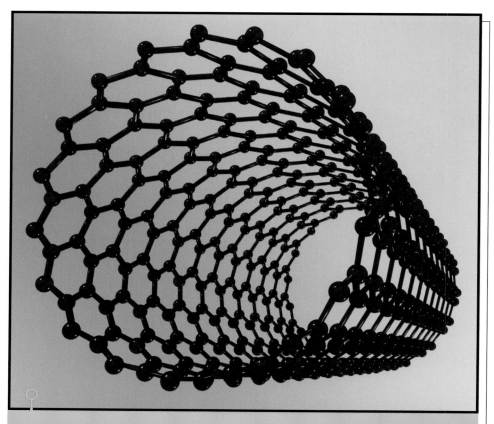

Carbon nanotubes are small. So small that the thickness of a strand of hair is around ten thousand times larger than the thickness of a typical carbon nanotube!

One example of nanotechnology that might change transistors is the carbon nanotube. This cylinder-shaped molecule of carbon is already being studied as a material for sensors, transistors, and lenses. Scientists are working with nanotubes to create an artificial retina. That part of the eye converts the image you see into electronic signals that are sent through nerves to the brain.

Researchers are working to fit billions of little nanotubes on an integrated circuit in a super computer. If it all seems too hard to believe, think about this: The first integrated circuits built in the 1950s had one transistor on each microchip. And that was considered groundbreaking. Modern computers use millions or billions of transistors on each chip.

How far and how small can we go with transistors? Who knows? But for a simple little device, it sure does provide some amazing possibilities.

USING A TRANSISTOR TO CONTROL AN LED

You know a transistor can pass along electric current when the base receives current and turns on the transistor. In this experiment, you're going to see how a smaller current can be used to control a larger current. You will build and test your own current amplifier using an NPN bipolar transistor. Most of these supplies should be available from an electronics store or online. Ask an adult for help with this experiment.

WHAT YOU'LL NEED

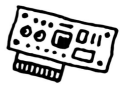

- six wires with alligator clips at each end
- one 470-ohm axial lead ⅛ or ¼ watt resistor
- one 9-volt battery
- one general purpose LED with a current rating of 20 mA
- a piece of paper and a writing utensil
- one NPN transistor, such as a PN2222 type or similar
- one 4700-ohm axial lead ⅛ or ¼ watt resistor

WHAT YOU'LL DO

1. Using one of the alligator clip wires, connect a wire from one end of the 470-ohm resistor to the positive terminal of the battery.
2. Using another alligator clip wire, connect a wire from the other end of the 470-ohm resistor to the long lead of the LED.
3. Connect a third wire from the short lead of the LED to the negative terminal of the battery.
4. Watch what happens, and record your findings.
5. Disconnect the third wire from the battery's negative terminal and connect it to the collector of the transistor. You can use the datasheet that comes with the transistor to identify the emitter, base, and collector.
6. Connect a fourth alligator clip wire from the emitter of the transistor to the negative terminal of the battery.
7. Watch what happens, and record your findings.
8. Now get the 4700-ohm resistor and use the fifth alligator clip wire to connect one end to the positive terminal of the battery.

9. Use the sixth alligator clip wire to connect the other end of the resistor to the base of the transistor.
10. Observe what happens, and record your findings.

FOLLOW-UP

Did the LED get brighter or dimmer when you added a transistor to the circuit? Based on what you've learned, why do you think that happened?

What happened to the LED when you used different types of resistors in the circuit? Based on what you've learned, what do you think is the purpose of the resistors in this type of circuit?

SOLVE IT! ANSWER KEY

HOW HEARING AIDS WORK (PAGE 10)

An amplifying transistor is what makes a hearing aid possible. In fact, hearing aids were the first commercial products to use transistors. In a hearing aid, sounds are picked up by a little microphone. Then they're sent as electric currents to a transistor that amplifies the power of those currents as it feeds them into a transmitter. The transmitter delivers the sounds in a much louder volume to the person wearing the hearing aid.

LED READING LIGHT (PAGE 18)

Depending on the other parts of your circuit, you could connect another battery to boost the current going through the LED. That would make it shine brighter. But since the sensor might be damaged by the additional current from an added battery, a better solution could be to add a transistor. Try connecting a transistor between the sensor and the LED in your circuit, since a transistor can turn a smaller current into a larger one. Make sure the current flows from the transistor to the LED and not the other way around.

amplify: to increase the current in an electronic device

base: the part of a transistor that controls the flow of electrons between the collector and the emitter. It's similar to a gate in a field-effect transistor.

bipolar transistor: a transistor used to amplify signals or switch currents and to make integrated circuits in computer chips. This is the most common type of transistor.

circuit: a path between at least two points that carries an electric current

collector: the part of a bipolar transistor that draws in current from the circuit before transmitting it to the emitter. It's similar to the source in a field-effect transistor.

component: any device or part of a circuit that affects the current

dope: to add elements or chemicals to a semiconductor material. The substances added to semiconductors are called dopants.

electric current: the flow of charged particles, usually electrons, in a circuit

emitter: the part of a bipolar transistor that releases current to the rest of the circuit. It's similar to the drain in a field-effect transistor.

field-effect transistor: a type of transistor that responds to voltage input. It is often used to amplify wireless electronic signals.

transistor: a device in an electric circuit that controls the current. A transistor can act as a switch or an amplifier.

SELECTED BIBLIOGRAPHY

"The Future of Transistors." *PBS*. Accessed December 1, 2015.
http://www.pbs.org/transistor/background1/events/transfuture.html.

"The History of the Integrated Circuit." Nobel Prize. Accessed December 4, 2015.
http://www.nobelprize.org/educational/physics/integrated_circuit/history/.

"The Transistor." Nobel Prize. Accessed December 4, 2015. http://www.nobelprize.org
/educational/physics/transistor/function/switching.html.

"Transistorized!" *PBS*. Accessed December 1, 2015. http://www.pbs.org/transistor
/album1/index.html.

Woodford, Chris. "Transistors." Explain That Stuff. Last modified May 9, 2015.
http://www.explainthatstuff.com/howtransistorswork.html.

FURTHER INFORMATION

Brain, Marshall. *The Engineering Book: From the Catapult to the Curiosity Rover; 250 Milestones in the History of Engineering.* New York: Sterling, 2015.
Check out the amazing solutions people have invented to overcome challenges in exploration, electronics, construction, and more.

Dossis, Nick. *Basic Electronics for Tomorrow's Inventors.* New York: McGraw-Hill, 2013.
Find out how to make your own gadgets while learning the essentials of electronics.

Leon, George deLucenay. *The Story of Electricity: With 20 Easy-to-Perform Experiments.* New York: Dover Publications, 2013. Kindle edition.
Re-create some of the most important electrical experiments in history.

Platt, Charles. *Make: Electronics.* 2nd ed. San Francisco: Maker Media, 2015.
Get some hands-on experience using transistors in real working circuits.

Roland, James. *How Circuits Work.* Minneapolis: Lerner Publications, 2016.
Learn more about what circuits are and how they power everything from a cell phone to a space station.

Timeline of Computer History
http://www.computerhistory.org/timeline/computers/
Find out how the computer age really took off after the invention of the transistor.

Transistors
https://learn.sparkfun.com/tutorials/transistors
Learn all the parts of a transistor and how different types of transistors work in a circuit.

PHOTO ACKNOWLEDGMENTS

The images in this book are used with the permission of: © iStockphoto. com/Sashatigar (robots and electrical microschemes); © iStockphoto. com/da-vooda (electronic icon); © iStockphoto.com/alenaZ0509 (zigzag background); © iStockphoto.com/Kubkoo, p. 1 (color dots); © iStockphoto. com/SerrNovik, p. 4; © jultud/Shutterstock.com, p. 7; © iStockphoto. com/pictograph, p. 8; Rob Schuster, pp. 9, 15, 16, 26; © Andrey Popov/ Dreamstime.com, p. 10 (hearing aid); © iStockphoto.com/vitsirisukodom, p. 10 (electric wire); © iStockphoto.com/Plus, p. 11; © iStockphoto.com/ vitranc, p. 12; © airobody/Shutterstock.com, pp. 17, 19; © iStockphoto. com/Norasit Kaewsai, p. 18; © iStockphoto.com/Boltenkoff, p. 20; © H. ARMSTRONG ROBERTS/ClassicStock/Alamy, p. 22; © Everett Historical/ Shutterstock.com, p. 23; © iStockphoto.com/leezsnow, p. 24; © NYPL NYPL/ Science Source/Getty Images, p. 25; AP Photo/I. INOUE, p. 28; © Dagmara_K/ Shutterstock.com, p. 31; © iStockphoto.com/Olga Reukova, p. 32.

Cover: © iStockphoto.com/UmbertoPantalone (tablet and phone); © iStockphoto.com/Kubkoo (color dots); © iStockphoto.com/alenaZ0509 (zigzag background); © iStockphoto.com/Sashatigar (robots and electrical microschemes); © iStockphoto.com/da-vooda (electronic icon).